G. SCHIRMER OPERA ANTHOLOGY

ARIAS FOR
BASS

Compiled and Edited by
Robert L. Larsen

ISBN 0-7935-0404-X

G. SCHIRMER, Inc.

Distributed by

Hal Leonard Publishing Corporation
7777 West Bluemound Road P.O. Box 13819 Milwaukee, WI 53213

ROBERT L. LARSEN, editor and compiler of this anthology series, brings to the project experience from both professional opera and the academic realm. He is founder and artistic director of one of America's major opera festivals, the critically acclaimed Des Moines Metro Opera, and since the company's founding in 1973 has been conductor and stage director for all of its main stage productions. Since 1965 he has also been chairman of the department of music at Simpson College in Indianola, Iowa, and during his tenure the department has received national recognition and awards for its serious and extensive program of operatic training for undergraduates. Dr. Larsen holds a bachelor's degree from Simpson College, a master's degree in piano performance from the University of Michigan, and a doctoral degree in opera conducting from Indiana University. He is highly regarded as an opera coach and accompanist, and has assisted in the training of many artists with significant operatic careers.

The editor wishes to dedicate these volumes to the memory of Douglas Duncan, colleague and friend.

Editorial Advisor: Richard Walters
Aria Text Editor and Translator: Martha Gerhart
Assistant Editors: Patrick Hansen, William Casey
Music Engraving: Sangji International

On the cover: "L'opéra de Paris" by Raoul Dufy
Used by permission of The Phillips Collection, Washington, D.C.

CONTENTS

FOREWORD

It has been a pleasure to reflect on the enormous repertory that the world of opera affords, and to choose from it a group of important and representative arias for soprano, mezzo-soprano, tenor, baritone, and bass to be included in these anthologies of opera arias.

In making these selections, I confess that I have not applied a constant criterion or standard, but rather have chosen to alter my perspective with each volume. All of these collections are intended to be of particular use to students and teachers of voice. Thus the soprano volume, for example, concentrates on lyric arias, rather than venturing very far into the rich material for coloratura, spinto, or dramatic voices.

The other volumes include the lyric arias most often sung by student voices, but also include other significant arias for a voice-type. For instance, I can't imagine a young baritone who would not be inspired by looking through the wonder of the Prologue from *I Pagliacci* within the confines of his practice room, or a tenor who doesn't anticipate with excitement the day when "Che gelida manina" may fit his voice like a glove. On the other hand, I have omitted some important repertory, such as many of the great Verdi baritone arias, because they are widely available, and are certainly the province of only the most experienced performer. Instead, I have chosen pieces of value not previously found in such collections, including arias in English for each voice-type.

Each aria has been painstakingly researched in preparing these new editions, creating what I believe will be an eminently credible and useful source for this music. There are countless incidents where notes or words have been corrected to create a more substantiated presentation than in previous editions. Throughout the collections, one will find many spots where traditional cadenzas are recommended. Appropriate appoggiaturas, as defined by conservative application of tradition, are indicated as well. There are instances where an entirely revised piano reduction, more representative of the full score, has been created.

These anthologies are for all of us who must remain students of our art throughout our lifetimes. I'm a vocal coach and opera conductor who believes firmly in exposing the gifted performer to the firmament, being sure that he or she understands that each star must be attained at its own special time, to be plucked and polished again and again throughout a musical career. Among these arias may be the first one ever studied, but if it's by someone destined to be a real singer, it will remain in mind and heart forever.

Robert L. Larsen
March, 1991

NOTES and TRANSLATIONS

Translator's Note

My aim in providing these "literal" translations was to give accurate line-by-line translations, as opposed to word-by-word translations. At the same time, the goal was to translate a true sense of the thought of each word or phrase.

In this format, therefore, the words on each line of original language text correspond to the words on each line of translation. Whenever, for contextual and idiomatic reasons, a line-by-line format into English is not possible, the printing is indented. In such cases, the whole idea of the indented foreign-language text segment corresponds to the whole idea of the indented English translation segment.

There are many antiquated and poetic word forms in opera texts which appear in various usages. In editing the aria texts various punctuation was discovered in various sources. When challenged by discrepancies, I have made justifiable choices for this edition. In some cases the punctuation has been modernized in the interest of clarity or consistency.

M. G.

NOTES and TRANSLATIONS

The arias are presented chronologically by year of first performance.

DIE ENTFÜHRUNG AUS DEM SERAIL
(The Abduction from the Seraglio)
1782
music by Wolfgang Amadeus Mozart
libretto by Gottlieb Stephanie the younger (after a libretto by Christoph Friedrich Bretzner)

O, wie will ich triumphiren

from Act III, scene 1
setting: Turkey, the 16th century; a square in front of the Pasha's palace, outside Osmin's house; midnight
character: Osmin

Pedrillo and Blonde, Belmonte and Constanze have been caught in their attempt to escape from the seraglio. Osmin, the major-domo of the court, gloats over his victory. When Belmonte offers to bribe him with gold, Osmin says he wants their heads, not their money, and proceeds to order them all to be sent before Pasha Selim.

O, wie will ich triumphiren,	*Oh, how I will exult*
wenn sie euch zum Richtplatz führen,	*when they lead you to the gallows*
und die Hälse schnüren zu.	*and tie the noose around your necks.*
Hüpfen will ich, lachen, springen,	*I will hop, laugh, jump,*
und ein Freudenliedchen singen;	*and sing a little song of joy;*
denn nun hab' ich vor euch Ruh'.	*for then I'll have peace from you.*
Schleicht nur säuberlich und	*No matter how stealthily and*
leise,	* quietly you prowl,*
ihr verdammten Harems-mäuse,	*you cursed harem mice,*
unser Ohr entdeckt euch schon;	*our ears will surely detect you;*
und eh' ihr uns könnt entspringen,	*and before you can escape from us,*
seht ihr euch in unsern Schlingen,	*you'll see yourselves in our traps*
und erhaschet euren Lohn.	*and catch what's coming to you.*

LE NOZZE DI FIGARO
(The Marriage of Figaro)
1786
music by Wolfgang Amadeus Mozart
libretto by Lorenzo da Ponte (after *La Folle Journée, ou Le Mariage de Figaro*, a comedy by Pierre Augustin Caron de Beaumarchais)

La vendetta

from Act I
setting: near Seville, the 17th century; the palace of Count Almaviva
character: Dr. Bartolo

Marcellina holds a contract which Figaro once signed, promising to marry her if he couldn't pay back a loan. The payment was never made, and Marcellina has engaged Don Bartolo as her lawyer. Bartolo swears that he will launch a campaign of vengeance that will assure her of victory.

The historical notes and synopses in this section are by the editor; translations are by Martha Gerhart.

Bene, io tutto farò;	Very well, I'll do all I can;
senza riserve,	without reservation,
tutto a me palesate.	reveal everything to me.
(Avrei pur gusto di dar in moglie	(I would certainly relish giving my old
la mia serva antica a chi	servant as wife to the one who
mi fece un dì rapir l'amica.)	once robbed me of my sweetheart.)
La vendetta, oh, la vendetta	Vengeance—oh, vengeance
è un piacer serbato ai saggi.	is a pleasure reserved for the wise.
L'obbliar l'onte, gli oltraggi	To forget disgrace and offenses
è bassezza, è ognor viltà.	is always dishonor and cowardice.
Coll'astuzia, coll'arguzia,	With shrewdness, with wit,
col giudizio, col criterio,	with wisdom, with discretion,
si potrebbe...	it could be possible...
il fatto è serio.	The matter is serious,
Ma credete, si farà.	but believe it—it will be done.
Se tutto il codice dovessi	If I should have to turn the whole
volgere,	legal code around,
se tutto l'indice dovessi leggere,	if I should have to read the whole index,
con un equivoco, con un sinonimo	with an ambiguity, with a synonym
qualche garbuglio si troverà.	some confusion will be found.
Tutta Siviglia conosce Bartolo—	All Seville knows Bartolo —
il birbo Figaro vinto sarà.	the rascal Figaro will be defeated.

Se vuol ballare

from Act I
setting: near Seville, the 17th century; the palace of Count Almaviva; Figaro and Susanna's new apartment, not yet completely furnished; morning
character: Figaro

Figaro, valet to Count Almaviva, has just discovered from Susanna that the trip to England which the Count plans to make with Figaro and his bride-to-be is probably designed so that the Count can lavish his attentions on Susanna. Left alone, Figaro muses that he has a few ideas of his own especially designed for his employer.

Bravo, signor padrone!	Bravo, lord master!
Ora incomincio a capir il mistero,	Now I begin to understand the mystery,
e a veder schietto	and to see clearly
tutto il vostro progetto;	your whole plan;
a Londra, è vero?	to London, really?
Voi ministro, io corriero,	You as minister, I as courier,
e la Susanna...	and Susanna...
secreta ambasciatrice.	secret ambassadress.
Non sarà, Figaro il dice!	That will not be — Figaro says so!
Se vuol ballare, signor contino,	If you want to dance, little lord count,
il chitarrino le suonerò, sì.	I'll play the guitar for you—yes.
Se vuol venire nella mia scuola,	If you want to come to my school,
la capriola le insegnerò, sì.	I'll teach you the caper — yes.
Saprò, ma piano;	I'll learn, but slowly;
meglio ogni arcano dissimulando	I'll be able to discover every secret
scoprir potrò.	better while playing the part.
L'arte schermendo, l'arte adoprando,	Defending my cunning, using my cunning,
di quà pungendo, di là scherzando,	stinging here, joking there,
tutte le macchine rovescierò.	I'll turn all your plots upside down.

Non più andrai

from Act I
setting: near Seville, the 17th century; the palace of Count Almaviva; Figaro and Susanna's new apartment, not yet completely furnished
character: Figaro

Count Almaviva, annoyed by the antics of the court page Cherubino, has consigned the boy to military duty. Susanna looks on as Figaro describes for him the joys and sorrows of a soldier's life.

Non più andrai, farfallone amoroso,	*You won't be flitting around anymore like*
notte e giorno d'intorno girando,	*a big amorous butterfly night and day*
delle belle turbando il riposo,	*disturbing the repose of beautiful women,*
Narcisetto, Adoncino d'amor.	*little Narcissus, little Adonis of love.*
Non più avrai questi bei pennacchini,	*You'll no longer have these pretty feathers,*
quel cappello leggiero e galante,	*that light and gallant hat,*
quella chioma, quell'aria brillante,	*that head of hair, that sparkling air,*
quel vermiglio donnesco color!	*that bright red womanish color!*
Non più avrai quei pennacchini,	*You'll no longer have those feathers,*
quel cappello, quella chioma,	*that hat, that head of hair,*
quell' aria brillante!	*that sparkling air!*
Fra guerrieri, poffar Bacco!	*Among soldiers, by Jove!*
Gran mustacchi, stretto sacco,	*Big mustache, tight tunic,*
schioppo in spalla, sciabla al fianco,	*gun on your shoulder, sabre at your side,*
collo dritto, muso franco,	*neck straight, face forward,*
un gran casco, o un gran turbante,	*a big helmet or a big turban,*
molto onor, poco contante.	*much honor, little cash.*
Ed invece del fandango	*And instead of the fandango,*
una marcia per il fango,	*a march through the mud...*
Per montagne, per valloni,	*over mountains, through glens,*
con le nevi, e i sollioni,	*in the snows and the hot suns,*
al concerto di tromboni, di bombarde,	*to the accompaniment of trombones, of bombards,*
di cannoni, che le palle	*of cannons that make the cannonballs,*
in tutti i tuoni,	*amidst all the thunder,*
all'orecchio fan fischiar.	*whistle in your ears.*
Cherubino, alla vittoria,	*Cherubino, to victory—*
alla gloria militar!	*to military glory!*

Aprite un po' quegl'occhi

from Act IV
setting: near Seville, the 17th century; the palace garden of Count Almaviva; night
character: Figaro

On the night of their wedding, Figaro believes that Susanna is deceiving him with the Count. Infuriated, he denounces all of womankind.

Tutto è disposto;	*Everything is ready;*
l'ora dovrebbe esser vicina.	*the hour must be near.*
Io sento gente... è dessa!	*I hear people... it's she!*
Non è alcun;	*It's no one.*
buja è la notte,	*The night is dark,*
ed io comincio omai a fare	*and I'm just beginning to practice*
il scimunito mestiere di marito.	*the idiotic profession of husband.*
Ingrata! Nel momento della mia	*Ungrateful girl! At the moment of my*
cerimonia ei godeva leggendo;	*ceremony he was enjoying reading;*
e nel vederlo, io rideva di	*and, seeing him, I laughed at*
me senza saperlo.	*myself without knowing it.*
O Susanna! quanta pena mi costi!	*Oh Susanna, how much pain you cost me!*
Con quell'ingenua faccia,	*With that ingenuous face,*
con quegl'occhi innocenti,	*with those innocent eyes,*
chi creduto l'avria?	*who would have believed it?*
Ah! che il fidarsi a donna	*Ah, how trusting in a woman*
è ognor follia.	*is always folly.*
Aprite un po' quegl'occhi,	*Open those eyes a bit,*
uomini incauti e sciocchi.	*rash and foolish men.*
Guardate queste femmine,	*Look at these women;*
guardate cosa son!	*see what they are!*
Queste chiamate dee, dagli ingannati	*Deceived by your senses, you call these*
sensi, a cui tributa incensi	*women goddesses, to whom weak reason*
la debole ragion.	*offers incense.*
Son streghe che incantano	*They are witches who charm*
per farci penar,	*in order to make us suffer,*
sirene che cantano	*sirens who sing*
per farci affogar,	*in order to make us drown,*
civette che allettano	*owls that allure*
per trarci le piume,	*in order to pull out our feathers,*
comete che brillano	*comets that shine*
per toglierci il lume;	*in order to blind us.*
son rose spinose,	*They are thorny roses;*
son volpi vezzose,	*they are graceful foxes.*

son orse benigne,	They are tame she-bears,
colombe maligne,	malicious doves,
maestre d'inganni,	mistresses of deception,
amiche d'affani,	friends of suffering
che fingono, mentono.	who fabricate, lie.
Amore non senton, non	They don't feel love; they don't
senton pietà, no.	feel pity - no.
Il resto nol dico,	I'm not saying the rest;
già ognuno lo sa.	every man already knows it.

DON GIOVANNI

1787
music by Wolfgang Amadeus Mozart
libretto by Lorenzo da Ponte (after Giovanni Bertati's libretto for Giuseppe Gazzinga's opera *Il convitato di pietra;* also after the Don Juan legends)

Madamina! Il catalogo è questo

from Act I, scene 2
setting: near Seville, the 17th century; a desolate road; early morning
character: Leporello

Returning from an evening in Seville, Giovanni and his servant Leporello encounter an attractive woman emerging from a coach. The Don amorously approaches her only to discover when she turns around that it is Donna Elvira, a woman he married in Burgos. As quickly as possible he slips away, leaving Leporello to tell her the truth about her husband by reading a list of his conquests.

Madamina! il catalogo è questo	My little lady, this is the catalogue
delle belle che amò il	of the beautiful women whom my master
padron mio;	has loved;
un catalogo egli è che ho fatt'io;	it's a list that I've made myself—
osservate, leggete con me!	look, read with me!
In Italia sei cento e quaranta,	In Italy six hundred and forty,
in Almagna due cento e trent'una,	in Germany two hundred and thirty-one;
cento in Francia, in Turchia novant'una;	a hundred in France, ninety-one in Turkey—
ma, in Ispagna son già mille e tre!	but, in Spain are already a thousand and three!
V'han fra queste contadine,	Among these there are country girls,
cameriere, cittadine,	chambermaids, city girls;
v'han contesse, baronesse,	there are countesses, baronesses,
marchesane, principesse,	marquises, princesses;
e v'han donne d'ogni grado,	and there are women of every rank,
d'ogni forma, d'ogni età.	of every shape, of every age.
Nella bionda egli ha l'usanza	To the blond he has the habit of
di lodarla la gentilezza,	extolling her kindness—
nella bruna la costanza,	to the brunette, her constancy,
nella bianca la dolcezza.	to the fair one, her sweetness.
Vuol d'inverno la grassotta,	In winter he wants the plump one;
vuol d'estate la magrotta,	in summer, he wants the skinny one
e la grande maestosa.	and the tall, stately one.
La piccina è ognor vezzosa;	The tiny one is always charming;
delle vecchie fa conquista,	the old ones he conquers
pel piacer di porle in lista.	for the pleasure of putting them on the list.
Sua passion predominante	His predominant passion
è la giovin principiante.	is the young beginner.
Non si picca, se sia ricca,	He takes no offense, be she rich,
se sia brutta, se sia bella,	be she ugly, be she beautiful;
purché porti la gonnella,	as long as she wears a skirt,
voi sapete quel che fa.	you know what he does.

DIE ZAUBERFLÖTE
(The Magic Flute)
1791
music by Wolfgang Amadeus Mozart
libretto by Emmanuel Schikaneder and Carl Giesecke (after a fairy tale by Wieland)

O Isis und Osiris

from Act II, scene 1
setting: Legendary; the Temple of Isis
character: Sarastro

In the inner courts of the Temple of Isis, priests assemble for solemn discussion and ritual. Sarastro, the high priest of the temple, invokes the blessing of the gods on Tamino and Pamina, who are to begin trials of initiation into the order.

O Isis und Osiris,	*Oh Isis and Osiris,*
schenket der Weisheit Geist	*bestow the spirit of wisdom*
dem neuen Paar!	*upon the new couple!*
Die ihr der Wandrer Schritte lenket,	*You who guide the steps of the travelers,*
stärkt mit Geduld sie in Gefahr.	*strengthen them with patience in peril.*
Laßt sie der Prüfung Früchte sehen,	*Let them see the fruits of the probation;*
doch sollten sie zu Grabe gehen,	*yet, must they go to the grave,*
so lohnt der Tugend kühnen Lauf,	*then reward the brave course of virtue:*
nehmt sie in euren Wohnsitz auf.	*receive them in your dwelling place.*

In diesen heil'gen Hallen

from Act II, scene 3
setting: Legendary; the palace of Sarastro
character: Sarastro

Sarastro enters to save Pamina from the evil Monostatos, who has threatened to kill her with the knife that her mother, the Queen of the Night, had given her to kill Sarastro. Pamina pleads with Sarastro not to punish her mother, and the priest responds in a spirit of benevolent conciliation.

In diesen heil'gen Hallen	*In these sacred halls*
kennt man die Rache nicht,	*one knows not revenge;*
und ist ein Mensch gefallen,	*and if a man has fallen,*
führt Liebe ihn zur Pflicht.	*love guides him to his obligation.*
Dann wandelt er an Freundes Hand	*Then he travels, by the hand of a friend,*
vergnügt und froh ins bess're Land.	*delighted and happy, to the better land.*
In diesen heil'gen Mauern,	*Within these sacred walls,*
wo Mensch den Menschen liebt,	*where man loves mankind,*
kann kein Verräter lauern,	*no traitor can lurk,*
weil man dem Feind vergibt.	*because one forgives the foe.*
Wen solche Lehren nicht erfreun,	*Whomever this teaching does not gladden*
verdienet nicht ein Mensch zu sein.	*does not deserve to be a man.*

IL BARBIERE DI SIVIGLIA
(The Barber of Seville)
1816
music by Gioachino Rossini
libretto by Cesare Sterbini (after *Le Barbier de Séville*, a comedy by Pierre Augustin Caron de Beaumarchais)

La calunnia

from Act I, scene 2
setting: Seville, the 17th century; a drawing room in the house of Dr. Bartolo
character: Dr. Bartolo.

Don Basilio, gossip and music teacher, tells Don Bartolo that Count Almaviva has been seen lurking in the neighborhood and that he believes him to be Bartolo's rival for the hand of Rosina. Basilio is sure that the situation can be handled by spreading suspicion and slander about the young man.

La calunnia è un venticello,	*Slander is a little wind,*
un'auretta assai gentile	*a very gentle little breeze*
che insensibile e sottile,	*which, imperceptibly and subtly,*
leggermente, dolcemente	*lightly, delicately*
incomincia a sussurrar.	*begins to whisper.*
Piano piano,	*Softly,*
terra terra,	*along the ground,*
sottovoce sibilando	*hissing under its breath*
va scorrendo,	*it goes gliding along,*
va ronzando;	*it goes buzzing along;*
nell'orecchie della gente	*it slips deftly into*
s'introduce destramente,	*peoples' ears*
e le teste ed i cervelli	*and stuns and inflates*
fa stordire e fa gonfiar.	*their heads and brains.*
Dalla bocca fuori uscendo	*Coming out of the mouth*
lo schiamazzo va crescendo;	*the hubbub starts to grow;*
prende forza a poco a poco,	*it gathers force little by little;*
vola già di loco in loco;	*now it flies hither and yonder;*
sembra il tuono,	*it seems like thunder,*
la tempesta che nel sen	*the storm that whistles*
della foresta va fischiando,	*and rumbles in the bosom of*
brontolando,	*the forest*
e ti fa d'orror gelar.	*and makes you freeze with horror.*
Alla fin trabocca e scoppia,	*In the end it overflows and bursts,*
si propaga, si raddoppia	*spreads, doubles,*
e produce un'esplosione	*and produces an explosion*
come un colpo di cannone,	*like a cannon shot,*
un tremuoto, un temporale,	*an earthquake, a thunderstorm —*
un tumulto generale	*a general turmoil*
che fa l'aria rimbombar.	*that makes the air resound.*
E il meschino calunniato,	*And the miserable slandered one —*
avvilito, calpestato,	*humiliated, trampled on —*
sotto il pubblico flagello	*under the public scourge*
per gran sorte va a crepar.	*by good fortune goes off to die.*

LA CENERENTOLA
or La Bontà in Trionfo
(Cinderella, or The Triumph of Goodness)
1817
music by Gioachino Rossini
libretto by Jacopo Ferretti (after Charles Guillaume Etienne's libretto for *Cendrillon* by Nicolas Isouard, also after the fairy tale)

Miei rampolli femminini

from Act I
setting: Salerno, time unspecified (c. 18th century); the house of Don Magnifico
character: Don Magnifico

Don Magnifico's daughters, Clorinda and Thisbe, have been quarreling loudly and manage to wake up their father. He blusters out of his chamber in his nightcap and dressing gown and tells them of the remarkable dream which their screaming has shattered.

Miei rampolli femminini,	*My female offspring,*
vi ripudio; mi vergogno!	*I disown you; I'm ashamed!*
Un magnifico mio sogno	*You've come to disrupt*
mi veniste a sconcertar.	*a magnificent dream of mine.*
Come son mortificate!	*How mortified they are —*
Degne figlie d'un barone!	*worthy daughters of a baron!*
Via: silenzio ed attenzione.	*Now then, be quiet and pay attention.*
State il sogno a meditar.	*Just ponder the dream.*
Mi sognai fra il fosco e il	*I dreamt, between darkness and*
chiaro un bellissimo somaro;	*light, of a most beautiful donkey —*
un somaro, ma solenne.	*a donkey, but majestic.*
Quando a un tratto,	*When all of a sudden —*
oh che portento!	*oh, what wonder—*
sulle spalle a cento a cento	*upon his shoulders, by the hundreds*
gli spuntavano le penne,	*there sprouted feathers,*
ed in aria, sciù, volò!	*and into the air — whoosh — he flew!*
Ed in cima a un campanile	*And on the top of a bell-tower,*
come in trono si fermò.	*as if on a throne, he stopped.*
Si sentiano per di sotto	*The bells could be heard ringing*
le campane a dindonar din, don...	*below — ding, dong...*
Col cì cì ciù ciù di botto	*With your yip yip yap yap suddenly*
mi veniste a risvegliar,	*you came to wake me up;*
col cì cì ciù ciù di botto	*with your yip yip yap yap suddenly*
mi faceste risvegliar.	*you made me wake up.*
Ma d'un sogno sì intralciato	*But of such an intricate dream*
ecco il simbolo spiegato.	*here is the symbolism explained:*
La campana suona a festa?	*The bell rings festively?*
Allegrezza in casa questa.	*Joy in this house.*
Quelle penne? Siete voi.	*Those feathers? They are you.*
Quel gran volo? Plebe addio.	*That great flight? Plebians, farewell.*
Resta l'asino di poi.	*Then there remains the ass.*
Ma quell'asino son io,	*But I am that ass —*
chi vi guarda vede chiaro	*anyone who looks at you can see clearly*
che il somaro è il genitor.	*that the donkey is your father.*
Fertilissima regina	*A most fertile queen*
l'una e l'altra diverrà;	*each of you will become;*
ed il nonno una dozzina di rampolli	*and the grandpa will embrace*
abbraccierà.	*a dozen offspring.*
Un re piccolo di qua... servo;	*A little king here... your servant;*
un re bambolo di là... servo;	*a baby king there... your servant;*
e la gloria mia sarà, sì,	*and the glory will be mine, yes!*
ed il nonno una dozzina di nipoti	*And the grandpa will embrace*
abbraccierà,	*a dozen grandchildren,*
e la gloria mia sarà.	*and the glory will be mine.*

DER FREISCHÜTZ

(The Free-shooter)

1821

music by Carl Maria von Weber

libretto by Friedrich Kind (after Gothic legend, and a story by Johann August Apel and Friedrich Laun)

Schweig'! schweig'! damit dich niemand warnt

from Act I

setting: Mythical, ancient Germany; a clearing before an inn in the forest

character: Caspar

Max is desperate to win the shooting contest on the morrow because the prize is the position of chief forester and the hand of his beloved Agathe. Max, one of the best marksmen in the county, seems to have lost his skill, and Caspar, already controlled by the Black Huntsman, has just persuaded Max to meet him in the Wolf's Glen at midnight to forge magic bullets. Caspar gloats that now the demons will have another victim.

Schweig'!	*Keep quiet —*
damit dich niemand warnt.	*so that nobody can warn you!*
Schweige!	*Quiet!*
Der Hölle Netz	*The net of hell*
hat dich umgarnt!	*has ensnared you!*
Nichts kann vom tiefen Fall	*Nothing can save you from the*
dich retten!	*abysmal fall!*
Umgebt ihn, ihr Geister	*Surround him, you spirits*
mit Dunkel beschwingt;	*winged with darkness;*
schon trägt er knirschend	*already he bears your*
eure Ketten!	*gnashing chains!*
Triumph!	*Victory!*
Die Rache gelingt!	*Revenge is succeeding!*

LA SONNAMBULA

(The Sleepwalker)
1831
music by Vincenzo Bellini
libretto by Felice Romani (after *La Sonnambule*, a ballet-pantomine by Eugène Scribe)

Vi ravviso

from Act I, scene 1
setting: a Swiss mountain village, the 19th century; the village square outside Lisa's inn
character: Count Rodolpho

Count Rodolpho, lord of the manor, who disappeared from his mountain village in Switzerland as a child, returns in an officer's uniform and asks directions from the villagers to the manor. They tell him that it is three miles beyond the village and that he should rest in the inn for the night. As he looks around at the mill, the fountain, and the fields, a flood of pleasant memories overtakes him.

Il mulino... il fonte... il bosco...	*The mill... the fountain... the woods...*
e vicin la fattoria!	*and the farmhouse nearby!*
Vi ravviso, o luoghi ameni,	*I see you again, oh pleasant surroundings*
in cui lieti, in cui sereni	*in which I so peacefully spent the*
sì tranquillo i dì passai	*happy and serene days*
della prima gioventù!	*of my early youth!*
Cari luoghi, io vi trovai,	*Dear surroundings, I've found you,*
ma quei dì non trovo più!	*but those days I find no more!*
Ma fra voi, se non m'inganno,	*But among you, if I'm not mistaken,*
oggi ha luogo alcuna festa?	*some celebration is taking place?*
E la sposa? è quella?	*And the bride — it is she?*
È gentil, leggiadra molto.	*She's refined, very charming.*
Ch'io ti miri!	*Let me look at you!*
Oh! il vago volto!	*Oh, the lovely face!*
Tu non sai con quei begli occhi	*You don't know how sweetly you touch my*
come dolce il cor mi tocchi,	*heart with those beautiful eyes,*
qual richiami ai pensier miei	*what an adorable beauty you recall*
adorabile beltà.	*to my thoughts.*
Era dessa, ah qual tu sei,	*That one was — ah, as you are —*
sul mattino dell'età, sì!	*in the morning of her years—yes!*

LUCIA DI LAMMERMOOR

(Lucy of Lammermoor)

1835

music by Gaetano Donizetti

libretto by Salvatore Cammarano (after Walter Scott's novel *The Bride of Lammermoor*)

Dalle stanze ove Lucia

from Act II, scene 1; or Act III, scene 1 (depending on the version)

setting: Scotland, c. 1702; a great hall in Lammermoor Castle

character: Raimondo Bidebent

Raimondo Bidebent, Lucia Ashton's tutor, interrupts the wedding festivities in honor of the marriage of Lord Arturo Bucklaw to Lucia. He solemnly tells the guests that, upon hearing a groan of anguish, he rushed to the bridal suite to find Lucia, with knife in hand, poised over the lifeless body of her husband.

Cessi, ah cessi quel contento.	*Cease, oh cease that joy.*
Cessi, cessi... Un fiero evento!	*Cease, cease... A cruel happening!*
Ah!	*Ah!*
Dalle stanze ove Lucia	*From the rooms where Lucia*
tratta avea col suo consorte,	*had withdrawn with her consort*
un lamento... un grido uscia,	*a lament... a cry emerged,*
come d'uom vicino a morte!	*as of a man near death!*
Corsi ratto in quelle mura...	*I ran quickly to within those walls...*
ahi! terribile sciagura!	*Ah, terrible disaster!*
Steso Arturo al suol giaceva	*Arturo was lying stretched out on the floor*
muto, freddo, insanguinato!	*mute, cold, bloody!*
e Lucia l'acciar stringeva,	*And Lucia was clasping the blade*
che fu già del trucidato!	*that was actually from the murdered one!*
Ella in me le luci affisse.	*She fixed her eyes on me.*
«Il mio sposo ov'è?» mi disse,	*"My husband—where is he?" she said to me;*
e nel volto suo pallente	*and on her pale face*
un sorriso balenò!	*a smile flashed!*
Infelice! della mente la virtude	*Unhappy one—her strength of mind*
a lei mancò! ah!	*was gone—ah!*
Ah! quella destra di sangue impura	*Ah, may that hand, impure with blood,*
l'ira non chiami su noi del ciel.	*not call the wrath of heaven upon us.*

LES HUGUENOTS

(The Huguenots)

1836

music by Giacomo Meyerbeer

libretto by Eugène Scribe and Emile Deschamps (after history)

Pour les couvents c'est fini (Piff, paff)

from Act I

setting: France, 1572; a banquet hall in the castle of Count de Nevers

character: Marcel

Marcel is the old servant of Raoul de Nangis, a young Huguenot nobleman who has just received a commission in the Lancers. The Count de Nevers has included Raoul in a social evening with his friends, all Catholic. To the embarrassment of Raoul, Marcel, a fanatical Huguenot, is outspoken in his contempt for them, and when they good-naturedly ask him to sing, he chooses the battle song of the Protestants at Rochelle—a denunciation of Papists, bigots, and women.

Volontiers,	Gladly:
un vieil air huguenot	an old Huguenot air
contre les gens du pape	against the servants of the pope
et le sexe damnable;	and the abominable sex;
vous le connaissez bien —	you know it well.
c'est notre air des combats,	It's our song of battle —
celui de la Rochelle:	the one from La Rochelle.
c'était alors	It was then
qu'au bruit des tambours,	that to the noise of the drums,
des cymbales,	of the cymbals,
accompagné du piff, paff, pouff	accompanied by the bang, bang, boom
des balles	of the bullets
je chantais:	I sang:
piff, paff.	bang, bang.
Pour les couvents c'est fini,	For the convents it's over;
les moines à terre;	the monks are felled.
guerre à tout cagot béni,	War to every blessed hypocrite;
papistes la guerre.	war to papists.
Livrons à la flamme aux fers	We'll deliver their temples of hell
leurs temples d'enfer;	to the blaze of swords;
terrassons-les, cernons-les,	let's knock them down, beseige them,
frappons-les, perçons-les,	strike them, run them through —
piff, paff, pouff.	bang, bang, boom.
Qu'ils pleurent,	Let them cry,
qu'ils meurent,	let them die;
mais grâce jamais,	but mercy — never,
non, jamais.	no, never.
Jamais mon bras ne trembla	Never will my arm tremble
aux plaintes des femmes.	at the moans of women.
Malheur à ces Dalilas	Woe to those Dalilas
qui perdent les âmes;	who lose their souls;
brisons au tranchant du fer	we'll break their infernal charms
leurs charmes d'enfer.	at the cutting of the sword.
Ces beaux démons, chassez-les,	Those fair demons — pursue them,
traquez-les, frappez-les,	round them up, strike them...
piff, paff, pouff.	bang, bang, boom.

DON PASQUALE

1843
music by Gaetano Donizetti
libretto by the composer and Giovanni Ruffini (after the libretto by Angeli Aneli for Stefano Pavesi's *Ser Marc' Antonio*)

Ah! un foco insolito

from Act I, scene 1
setting: Rome, the 19th century; the house of Don Pasquale
character: Don Pasquale

Dr. Malatesta has just told his friend Don Pasquale that he has a sister who would be perfect for him as a bride. Old Pasquale is delighted and orders Malatesta to go immediately and bring her to him. Then he proceeds to anticipate with glee the new life in store for him as a husband and father.

Ah! un foco insolito mi sento addosso,	Ah, I feel a strange fire inside me;
omai resistere io più non posso.	now I can't resist anymore!
Dell'età vecchia scordo i malanni,	I forget the woes of old age;
mi sento giovine come a vent'anni.	I feel like a young man of twenty.
Deh! cara, affrettati!	Please, dear, hurry!
Vieni, sposina!	Come, little bride!
Ecco, di bamboli mezza dozzina	Look, I already see half a dozen children
già veggo nascere, crescere,	being born, growing up,
a me d'intorno veggo scherzar.	playing around me.
Vieni, chè un foco insolito	Come, because I feel a strange fire
mi sento addosso,	inside me,
o casco morto qua.	or else I'll drop dead here.
Deh! vieni, affrettati, bella sposina!	Please—come, hurry, beautiful little wife!
Già di bamboli mezza dozzina	I already see half a dozen children
a me d'intorno veggo scherzar.	playing around me.

ERNANI

1844
music by Giuseppe Verdi
libretto by Francesco Maria Piave (after Victor Hugo's play *Hernani*)

Infelice! e tuo credevi

from Act I
setting: Spain, c. 1519; the castle of Don Ruy Gomez de Silva, grandee of Spain; Elvira's apartment
character: Don Ruy Gomez de Silva

Elvira is a kinswoman to the aged Don Ruy Gomez de Silva, whom she is pledged to marry. She is, however, in love with the bandit chief Ernani who is really the disguised John of Aragon. Don Carlos, King of Castile, also loves Elvira and has observed the signal with which Ernani gains admission to Elvira's apartments. He imitates it and enters, but after having been repulsed by Elvira and trying to drag her away, he is stopped by Ernani, who emerges through a secret panel. Silva suddenly enters and expresses horror in finding two men in his lady's rooms.

Che mai vegg'io!	*Whatever do I see!*
Nel penetral più sacro di mia magione;	*In the most sacred chamber of my dwelling,*
presso a lei, che sposa esser dovrà	*near her, who is to be the bride*
d'un Silva,	*of a Silva,*
due seduttori io scorgo?	*I discover two seducers?*
Entrate, olà, miei fidi cavalieri.	*Enter, you there, my faithful cavaliers.*
Sia ognun testimon del disonore,	*May each be witness to the dishonor,*
dell'onta che si reca al	*to the shame that is being brought to*
suo signore.	*his lord.*
Infelice! e tuo credevi sì bel	*Unhappy man, you believed such a beautiful*
giglio immacolato!	*lily of yours to be chaste?*
Del tuo crine fra le nevi	*Among the snows of your hair*
piomba invece il disonor.	*falls, instead, dishonor.*
Ah, perché l'etade in seno	*Ah, why has age preserved a youthful*
giovin core m'ha serbato!	*heart in my breast?*
Mi dovevan gli anni almeno	*The years should at least*
far di gelo ancora il cor.	*have turned my heart to ice.*

MACBETH

1847
music by Giuseppe Verdi
libretto by Francesco Maria Piave (after the tragedy by William Shakespeare)

Come dal ciel precipita

from Act II, scene 2
setting: Scotland, 1040; a park near Duncan's castle; night
character: Banco (Banquo in Shakespeare)

Unaware that assassins are gathering about him, Banco, one of Macbeth's generals, enters a park near the castle with his son Fleance at night. At the conclusion of the aria Banco is murdered, but his son escapes.

Studia il passo, o mio figlio!	*Watch your step, oh my son!*
Usciam da queste tenebre;	*Let us leave this darkness.*
un senso ignoto nascer mi sento	*I feel rising in my breast*
in petto,	*a strange feeling*
pien di tristo presagio	*full of ill omen*
e di sospetto.	*and of suspicion.*
Come dal ciel precipita l'ombra	*How the shadows fall from the sky*
più sempre oscura!	*ever more dark!*
In notte ugual trafissero Duncano,	*On such a night they slew Duncan,*
il mio signor.	*my lord.*
Mille affannose immagini	*A thousand troubled images*
m'annunciano sventura,	*prophesy misfortune to me*
e il mio pensiero ingombrano	*and encumber my thoughts*
di larve e di terror.	*with apparitions and terror.*

DIE LUSTIGEN WEIBER VON WINDSOR

(The Merry Wives of Windsor)
1849
music by Otto Nicolai
libretto by Hermann von Mosenthal (after the comedy by William Shakespeare)

Als Büblein klein

from Act II, scene 1
setting: Windsor, England, c. 1600; the Garter Inn
character: Sir John Falstaff

Sir John Falstaff sits amidst his cronies at the Garter Inn drinking sack and trying to dry out from his dunking in the river Thames in a laundry basket. The text is a parody of the clown's final song from *Twelfth Night*.

Als Büblein klein an der Mutter Brust,	*When a tiny little boy at my mother's breast—*
hopp heisa bei Regen und Wind,	*heigh-ho in the rain and the wind—*
da war der Sekt schon meine Lust,	*then sparkling wine was already my pleasure,*
denn der Regen der regnet jeglichen Tag!	*for the rain, it rained every day!*
Komm, braune Hanne, her,	*Come here, tawny Jane—*
reich mir die Kanne her,	*pass me the jug,*
füll' mir den Schlauch!	*fill my flask!*
Lösch' mir der Kehle Brand.	*Quench my parched throat.*
Trinken ist keine Schand';	*Drinking is no disgrace;*
Bachus trank auch, ja!	*Bacchus drank too, of course!*
Nun in Positur!	*Now on your mark!*
Haltet Euch bereit!	*Ready, get set!*
Macht die Kehlen weit!	*Open your throats wide!*
Eins, zwei und drei.	*One, two and three.*
Und als ich vertreten die Kinderschuh',	*And when I outwore my childhood shoes—*
hopp heisa bei Regen und Wind,	*heigh-ho in the rain and the wind—*
da schloßen die Mädel sich vor mir zu,	*then the girls locked themselves in from me,*
denn der Regen der regnet jeglichen Tag!	*for the rain, it rained every day!*
Und ist die Tasche leer,	*And if the pocket is empty,*
und wird die Flasche leer,	*and the bottle becomes empty,*
kommt Würfel raus!	*out come the dice!*
Glück ist ein spröder Gast;	*Good fortune is a stubborn guest;*
wer es beim Schopfe faßt,	*the one who grabs it by the neck*
führt es nach Haus, ja!	*leads it home—yes!*

I VESPRI SICILIANI (LES VÊPRES SICILIENNES)

(The Sicilian Vespers)
1855
music by Giuseppe Verdi
libretto by Eugène Scribe and Charles Duveyrier (after their libretto for Donizetti's opera *Le Duc d'Albe*, which was based on history)

note: The Italian translation by Fusinato and Caimi has become standard.

O tu, Palermo

from Act II
setting: A valley near the city of Palermo, 1282
character: Giovanni da Procida

Giovanni da Procida is a Sicilian doctor who, until his banishment, was the leader of the Sicilian patriots opposing French domination. He has secretly returned to stir up the resistance movement, and wanders in a valley outside of the city of Palermo, extolling his beloved native land.

O patria, o cara patria,
alfin ti veggo!
L'esule ti saluta
dopo sì lunga assenza.
Il fiorente tuo suolo
    ripien d'amore io bacio,
reco il mio voto a te
col braccio e il core!

O tu, Palermo, terra adorata,
a me sì caro riso d'amor, ah!
alza la fronte tanto oltraggiata,
il tuo ripiglia primier splendor!
Chiesi aita a straniere nazioni,
ramingai per castella e città;
ma insensibil al fervido sprone
dicea ciascun:
Siciliani, ov'è il prisco valor?
Su, sorgete a vittoria, all'onor!
Ah, torna al primiero almo splendor!

Oh fatherland, oh dear fatherland,
at last I see you!
The exile greets you
after such a long absence.
Full of love, I kiss
    your flowering soil;
I bring my vow to you
with my arms and my heart!

Oh you, Palermo, adored ground,
light of love so dear to me — ah,
raise your brow, so much abused;
recapture your former splendor!
I called to foreign nations for help —
I roved through castles and cities;
but, indifferent to my impassioned spur,
everyone said:
Sicilians, where is your courage of old?
Come, rise to victory, to honor!
Ah, return to your former noble splendor!

SIMON BOCCANEGRA

1857
music by Giuseppe Verdi
libretto by Francesca Maria Piave and Arrigo Boito

Il lacerato spirito

from the prologue
setting: Genoa, the 14th century; a square before the Church of San Lorenzo, near the palace of Jacopo Fiesco; night
character: Jacopo Fiesco

Jacopo Fiesco, a nobleman of Genoa, mourns the death of his daughter Maria, whom he had virtually imprisoned in his palace after she had an affair with the commoner Simon Boccanegra and bore him a child.

A te l'estremo addio,
palagio altero,
freddo sepolcro dell'angiolo mio!
Nè a proteggerlo valsi!
Oh maledetto!
Oh vile seduttore!
E tu, Vergin, soffristi rapita
    a lei la verginal corona?
Ah! che dissi? deliro!
Ah! mi perdona!

Il lacerato spirito
del mesto genitore
era serbato a strazio
d'infamia e di dolore.
Il serto a lei de' martiri
    pietoso il cielo diè.
Resa al fulgor degli angeli,
prega, Maria, per me.

To you my last farewell,
proud palace,
cold sepulchre of my angel!
I was worth nothing in protecting her!
Oh cursed man!
Oh vile seducer!
And you, Virgin — you let her be
    robbed of her virginal crown?
Ah, what have I said? I'm raving!
Ah, forgive me!

The broken spirit
of the sad father
was reserved for the agony
of infamy and of sorrow.
Heaven mercifully bestowed upon her
    the wreath of martyrs.
Returned to the radiance of the angels,
pray, Maria, for me.

FAUST

1859
music by Charles Gounod
libretto by Jules Barbier and Michel Carré (after the drama by Johann Wolfgang von Goethe)

Le veau d'or

from Act II (often performed as Act I, scene 2)
setting: a village in Germany, the 16th century; the village square
character: Méphistophélès

Soldiers and townspeople are gathered on the eve of the troops' departure on a campaign. Wagner, a young student, is holding forth with his "Song of the Rat" when Méphistophélès suddenly appears and interrupts the proceedings by singing his profane "Song of the Golden Calf."

Le veau d'or est toujours debout!	*The calf of gold is still standing!*
On encense sa puissance	*People worship its power*
d'un bout du monde à l'autre bout!	*from one end of the world to the other!*
Pour fêter l'infâme idole,	*To celebrate the infamous idol,*
rois et peuples confondus,	*kings and commoners alike,*
au bruit sombre des écus,	*at the heavy thud of coins,*
dansent une ronde folle,	*dance a mad circle*
autour de son piédestal!	*around its pedestal!*
Et Satan conduit le bal!	*And Satan leads the dance!*
Le veau d'or est vainqueur des dieux!	*The calf of gold is vanquisher of the gods!*
Dans sa gloire dérisoire	*In his derisive glory*
le monstre abject insulte aux cieux!	*the vile monster insults the heavens!*
Il contemple, ô rage étrange! à ses	*He contemplates—oh fearsome mania—*
pieds le genre humain,	*the human race at his feet*
se ruant, le fer en main,	*throwing itself, sword in hand,*
dans le sang et dans la fange,	*into the blood and into the filth*
où brille l'ardent métal!	*where the burning metal glitters!*
Et Satan conduit le bal!	*And Satan leads the dance!*

Vous qui faites l'endormie

from Act IV, scene 3 (often performed as Act III, scene 3)
setting: a village in Germany, the 16th century; a square near the cathedral
character: Méphistophé!ès

Faust, accompanied by Méphistophélès, returns to Marguerite's house to see once more the girl he has dishonored and who carries his child. The devil throws back his cloak, strums his mandolin, and sings a diabolical parody of a lover's serenade.

Vous qui faites l'endormie,	*You who are pretending to be asleep,*
n'entendez-vous pas,	*don't you hear,*
ô Catherine, ma mie,	*oh Catherine, my love,*
ma voix et mes pas?	*my voice and my steps?*
Ainsi ton galant t'appelle,	*Thus does your suitor call you,*
et ton cœur l'en croit.	*and your heart gives in to him.*
Ah! ah! ah! ah!	*Ah! ah! ah! ah!*
N'ouvre ta porte, ma belle,	*Don't open your door, my beautiful one,*
que la bague au doigt!	*without the ring on your finger!*
Catherine que j'adore,	*Catherine, whom I adore,*
pourquoi refuser	*why refuse*
à l'amant qui vous implore	*to the lover who implores you*
un si doux baiser?	*so sweet a kiss?*
Ainsi ton galant supplie,	*Thus does your suitor beseech you,*
et ton cœur l'en croit.	*and your heart gives in to him.*
Ah! ah! ah! ah!	*Ah! ah! ah! ah!*
Ne donne un baiser, ma mie,	*Don't grant a kiss, my love,*
que la bague au doigt!	*without the ring on your finger!*
Ah! ah! ah! ah! ah! ah!	*Ah! ah! ah! ah! ah! ah!*

LA JOLIE FILLE DE PERTH
(The Fair Maid of Perth)
1867
music by Georges Bizet
libretto by J.H. Vernoy de St. Georges and Jules Adenis (after the novel by Sir Walter Scott)

Quand la flamme de l'amour

from Act II
setting: Perth, Scotland, the 19th century
character: Ralph

Henry Smith is in love with Catherine Glover in this tale drawn from Sir Walter Scott. Ralph is also enamored of Catherine, whom he thinks he sees being abducted by the Duke of Rothsay. He sings this drinking song about hopeless love just before telling Henry what he has seen.

La la la!... tra la la!... tra la!	*La la la!... tra la la!... tra la!*
Quand la flamme de l'amour	*When the flame of love*
brûle l'âme nuit et jour,	*burns the soul night and day,*
pour l'éteindre quelquefois,	*to quench it sometimes,*
sans me plaindre, moi je bois!	*without complaining, me—I drink!*
Je ris! Je chante!	*I laugh! I sing!*
Je ris, je chante et je bois!	*I laugh, I sing, and I drink!*
Tra la la la la! Ah! tra la la!...	*Tra la la la la! Ah! tra la la!...*
S'il est une triste folie,	*If there exists a sorry folly,*
c'est celle d'un pauvre amoureux	*it's that of a poor lover*
qu'un regard de femme humilie,	*whom a woman's glance humbles...*
qu'un mot peut rendre malheureux,	*whom a word can make unhappy—*
hélas!	*alas!*
Quand on aime sans espoir,	*When one loves without hope,*
le ciel même devient noir.	*heaven itself becomes gloomy.*
Eh! l'hôtesse... mon flacon!	*Hey, hostess... my bottle,*
que j'y laisse ma raison!	*so that I may leave my reason in it!*
Tra la la la la!...	*Tra la la la la!...*

EUGENE ONEGIN
1879
music by Pyotr Il'yich Tchaikovsky
libretto by Konstantin Shilovsky and the composer (after a poem by Alexander Pushkin)

Lyubvi vse vozrasty kokorny
(Gremin's aria)

from Act III, scene 1
setting: St. Petersburg, the late 19th century; a luxurious ballroom in the home of Prince Gremin
character: Prince Gremin

At a glittering reception in the home of Prince Gremin, the solitary Eugene Onegin, who has just returned to Russia from his aimless travels, sees Tatiana, whom he once rejected, now an elegant and gracious lady of society. He asks his host about her and Prince Gremin replies that the lady is his beloved wife.

Russian transliteration and translation by Lilia Guimaraev.

Ljubvi vse vozrasty pokorny,	*All ages are to love submissive,*
eja poryvy blagotvorny	*its impulses are beneficial*
i junoshe v rastsvete let,	*to blossoming youth,*
edva uvidevshemy svet,	*barely having seen the world.*
i zakalënnomu sud'boj	*and to those hardened by fate,*
bojtsu s sedoju golovoj!	*the gray-headed warrior!*
Onegin, ja skryvat' ne stanu,	*Onegin, I will not conceal,*
bezumno ja ljulju Tat'janu!	*madly I love Tatiana!*
Tosklivo zhizn' moja tekla,	*Drearily my life flowed,*
ona javilas' i dala,	*she appeared and gave,*
kak solntsa luch sredi nenast'ja,	*like a sun's ray in foul weather,*
mne zhizn' i molodost', da,	*life to me, and youth, yes,*
molodost', i schast'je!	*youth and happiness!*
Sredi lukavykh, malodushnykh,	*Amidst the sly, the faint-hearted,*
shal'nykh, balovannykh detej,	*the mad the spoiled children,*
zlodeev i smeshnykh,	*the scoundrels and the absurd,*
i skuchnukh,	*and the dull,*
tupykh, privjazchivykh sudej;	*the obtuse, the quick to judge;*
sredi koketok bogomol'nykh,	*amidst the religious coquettes,*
sredi kholpop'ev dobrovol'nykh,	*amidst the voluntary slaves,*
sredi vsednevnykh modnykh stsen,	*amidst the everyday stylish scenes,*
uchtivykh, laskovykh izmen;	*courteous, affectionate betrayal;*
sredi kholodnykh prigovorov	*amidst the frigid verdicts*
zhestokoserdoj suety,	*of cruel-hearted vanity,*
sredi dosadnoj pustoty	*amidst the annoying emptiness of*
razchetov, dum	*calculations, thoughts*
i razgovorov,	*and conversations,*
ona blistaet, kak zvezda	*she shines, like a star*
vo mrake nochi, v nebe chistom,	*in the gloom of night, in the clear sky,*
i mne javljaetsja vsegda	*and appears to me always*
v sijan'i angela,	*in the aureole of an angel,*
v sijan'i angela luchistom!	*radiant in the aureole of an angel!*
Ljubvi vse vozrasty pokorny,	*All ages are to love submissive,*
eja poryvy blagotvorny	*its impulses are beneficial*
i junoshe v rastsvete let,	*to blossoming youth,*
edva uvidevshemy svet,	*barely having seen the world,*
i zakalënnomy sud'boj	*and to those hardened by fate,*
bojtsu s sedoju golovoj.	*the gray-headed warrior.*
Onegin, ja skryvat' ne stanu,	*Onegin, I will not conceal,*
Bezumno ja ljublju Tat'janu!	*madly I love Tatiana!*
Tosklivo zhizn' moga tekla	*Drearily my life flowed,*
ona javilas' i dala,	*she appeared and gave,*
kak soln'tsa luch, sredi nenast'ja,	*like sun's ray in foul weather*
i zhizn, i molodost', da,	*life to me, and youth, yes,*
molodost' i schast'e,	*youth and happiness,*
i zhizn' i molodost' i schast'e!	*life and youth and happiness!*

MANON

1884
music by Jules Massenet
libretto by Henri Meilhac and Philippe Gille (after *L'Histoire du Chevalier des Grieux et de Manon Lescaut,* a novel by Abbé Prévost)

Épouse quelque brave fille

from Act III, scene 2 (often played as Act II, scene 2)
setting: Paris, 1721; the Seminary of St. Sulpice
character: Count Des Grieux

The Chevalier Des Grieux has just delivered his first sermon as an Abbé at the church of St. Sulpice. His father, the Count Des Grieux, has come for the service and mildly congratulates him, but his true motive in coming is to urge his son to renounce the church and find some suitable girl to marry.

22

Les grands mots que voilà!
Quelle route as-tu donc suivie,
et que sais-tu de cette vie
pour penser qu'elle finit là?

Épouse quelque brave fille
digne de nous, digne de toi;
deviens un père de famille
ni pire, ni meilleur que moi:
le ciel n'en veut pas davantage.
C'est là le devoir,
entends-tu?
C'est là le devoir!
La vertu qui fait du tapage
n'est déjà plus de la vertu!

What lofty words those are!
What path have you followed, then,
and what do you know about this life
to think that it ends with this?

Marry some fine girl
worthy of us, worthy of you;
become a family father
neither worse nor better than I:
heaven wishes no more.
Your obligation is there—
do you understand?
Your obligation is there!
Virtue which is ostentatious
is already no longer virtue!

LA BOHÈME

(The Bohemian Life)
1896
music by Giacomo Puccini
libretto by Giuseppe Giacoso and Luigi Illica (after the novel *Scènes de la Vie de Bohème* by Henri Murger)

Vecchia zimarra, senti

from Act IV
setting: Paris, c. 1830; a garret apartment
character: Colline

Musetta has brought Mimi, dying of consumption, to the apartment of the "bohemians." Musetta goes off with Marcello to sell her earrings and seeks medical help. Colline, the philosopher, says a gentle farewell to his old coat before taking it to the pawnbroker.

Vecchia zimarra, senti,
io resto al pian,
tu ascendere il sacro monte or devi.
Le mie grazie ricevi.
Mai non curvasti il logoro dorso
ai ricchi ed ai potenti.
Passar nelle tue tasche
  come in antri tranquilli
  filosofi e poeti.
Ora che i giorni lieti fuggir,
ti dico addio, fedele amico mio,
addio.

Shabby old overcoat, listen—
I am staying on the ground;
you must now ascend to the sacred mountain.*
Receive my thanks.
You never bowed your worn back
to the rich and the powerful.
Through your pockets, as if in tranquil
  dens, philosophers and poets have
  passed.
Now that happy days have fled,
I say farewell to you, my faithful friend—
farewell.

* A pun: in Italy, "monte di pietà" ("mountain of mercy") is a pawnshop.

STREET SCENE

1947
music by Kurt Weill
book by Elmer Rice, lyrics by Langston Hughes (based on the play by Elmer Rice)

Let things be like they always was
(Frank's aria)

from Act I
setting: A sidewalk in New York City, the present (1947); an evening in June
character: Frank Maurrant

Frank Maurrant lives with his wife and two children, Rose and little Willie, in a walk-up apartment in a lower class neighborhood of New York City. Frank is a strong, ordinary kind of a guy, uncomfortable with the foreigners who live around him. He has just had a violent discussion with his neighbor, Mr. Kaplan, about socialistic reforms, and his words in the aria may also hint at a vague awareness of his wife's unfaithfulness.

THE MOTHER OF US ALL

1947
music by Virgil Thomson
text by Gertrude Stein

What what is it?

from Act II, scene 2
setting: 19th century America; the drawing room of Susan B. Anthony
character: Daniel Webster

Daniel Webster strides on stage and tells Susan B. Anthony that she is far too impatient and lacks a broader vision. Suffrage for women need not be hastened. It is only a step along the road of progress to America's glory.

O, wie will ich triumphiren

from
DIE ENTFÜHRUNG AUS DEM SERAIL

Wolfgang Amadeus Mozart

OSMIN:

O, wie will ich tri - um - phi - ren, wenn sie euch zum Richt-platz füh - ren,

O, wie will ich tri - um - phi - ren, wenn sie euch zum Richt-platz

füh - ren, und die Häl - se schnü-ren zu, schnü-ren zu,

und die Häl - se schnü-ren zu, schnü - ren zu. Schleicht

nur säu - ber-lich und lei - se, ihr ver - damm - ten

Ha - rems - mäu - se, un - ser Ohr ent - deckt euch

schon; und eh' ihr uns könnt ent - sprin - gen, seht ihr euch in un - sern

Schlin - gen, und er - ha - schet eu - ren Lohn, und er - ha -

schet eu - ren Lohn.

29

Schleicht nur säu - ber - lich und lei - se, ihr ver -

damm - ten Ha - rems - mäu - se, un - ser Ohr ent - deckt euch

schon, ent - deckt euch schon, ent - deckt euch schon.

O, wie will ich tri - um - phi - ren, wenn sie euch zum Richt-platz

füh - ren, und die Häl - se schnü - ren zu, schnü - ren zu,

und die Häl - se schnü - ren zu, schnü - ren zu. Hüp - fen

will ich, la - chen, sprin - gen, und ein

Freu - den - lied - chen sin - - -

gen; denn nun hab' ich vor euch Ruh', denn nun hab' ich

vor euch Ruh'.

O, wie

will ich tri - um - phi - ren, wenn sie euch zum Richt-platz füh - ren,

und die Häl - se schnü-ren zu, schnü - ren zu, schnü - ren

schnü - ren, schnü-ren, schnü - ren, schnü - ren zu, und die Häl - se

cresc.

schnü - ren zu, und die Häl - se schnü - ren zu, und die Häl - se schnü - ren

f

zu, schnü-ren zu, schnü - ren zu.

La vendetta

from
LE NOZZE DI FIGARO

Wolfgang Amadeus Mozart

Be - ne, io tut - to fa - rò; sen - za ri - ser - ve, tut - to a me pa - le -

sa - te. (A-vrei pur gu-sto di dar in mo-glie la mia ser - va an - ti-ca a chi mi fe-ce un

dì ra-pir l'a-mi-ca.) La ven - det - ta, oh, la ven -

*Appoggiatura recommended

det - ta   è un   pia - cer ser - ba - to ai

sag - gi,   è un   pia - cer   ser - ba - to ai sag-gi.

L'ob - bli - ar _____ l'on - te, gli ol - trag - gi,   l'ob-bli-

ar _____ l'on - te, gli ol-trag - gi   è   bas - sez - za,   è o-

gu - zia, col giu - di - zio, col cri - te - rio, si po - treb - be, si po -

treb - be, si po - treb - be, si po - treb - be... il fat - to è

se - rio, il fat - to è se - rio, il fat - to è se - rio.

Ma cre - de - te, si fa - rà, ma cre -

leg - ge - re, con un e-qui-vo-co, con un si - no-ni- mo qual-che gar-bu - glio si tro-ve -

rà, qual - che gar - bu - glio_____ si tro - ve -

rà, si tro - ve - rà. Tut - ta Si-

vi - glia co - no - sce Bar - to-lo—— il bir - bo

Fi - ga-ro vin - to sa - rà, tut - ta Si - vi - glia

co - no - sce Bar - to - lo— il bir - bo Fi - ga - ro

vin - to sa - rà, il bir - bo Fi - ga - ro vin - to sa -

rà, il bir - bo Fi - ga - ro vin - to sa - rà,

cresc.

vin - to sa - rà,

vin - to sa - rà,

vin - to sa - rà.

Se vuol ballare

from
LE NOZZE DI FIGARO

Wolfgang Amadeus Mozart

*Appoggiatura recommended

44

se - cre-ta am-ba-scia-tri - ce. Non sa - rà, non sa-rà, Fi - ga-ro il di - ce!

Allegretto

Se vuol bal - la - re, si - gnor con - ti - no, se vuol bal-

p *staccato*

la - re, si - gnor con - ti - no, il chi - tar - ri - no le

suo - ne - rò, il chi - tar - ri - no le suo - ne-

rò, sì, le suo - ne - rò, sì, le suo - ne - rò.

Se vuol ve - ni - re

nel - la mia scuo - la, la ca - pri - o - la

le in - se - gne - rò. Se vuol ve - ni - re nel - la mia

pia - no, pia - no, pia - no, pia - no, pia - no, pia - no;

me - glio o - gni ar - ca - no

dis - si - mu - lan - do sco - prir po - trò.

Presto

L'ar - te scher - men - do, l'ar - te a - do - pran - do,

tut - te le mac - chi - ne ro - ve-scie - rò, tut - te le

mac - chi - ne ro - ve - scie - rò, tut - te le mac - chi - ne

ro - ve-scie - rò, ro - ve - scie - rò, ro - ve - scie - rò.

[Tempo I°]

Se vuol bal - la - re, si - gnor con - ti - no,

Non più andrai

from
LE NOZZE DI FIGARO

Wolfgang Amadeus Mozart

54

fran - co, un gran ca - sco, o un gran tur - ban - te, mol-to o -

nor, po - co con - tan - te, po - co con - tan - te, po - co con - tan - te. Ed in -

ve - ce del fan - dan - go u - na

mar - cia per il fan - go. Per mon - ta - gne, per val -

lo - ni, con le ne - vi, e i sol - lio - ni, al con - cer - to di trom -

bo - ni, di bom - bar - de, di can - no - ni, che le pal - le in tut - ti i

tuo - ni, all' o - rec - chio fan fi - schiar. Non più a -

vrai quei pen - nac - chi - ni, non più a -

bi - no, al-la vit - to - ria, al - la glo - ria mi - li - tar, al - la

glo - ria mi - li - tar, al - la glo - ria mi - li - tar!

Aprite un po' quegl'occhi

from
LE NOZZE DI FIGARO

Recitativo
FIGARO:

Tut-to è di-spo-sto; l'o-ra do-vreb-be es-ser vi-ci-na. Io sen-to

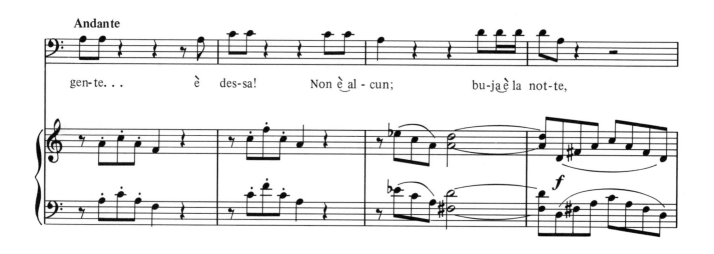

Andante

gen-te. . . è des-sa! Non è al-cun; bu-ja è la not-te,

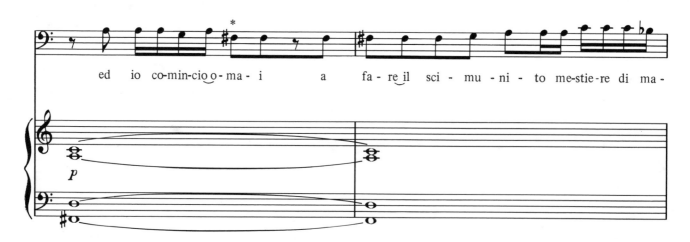

ed io co-min-cio o-ma-i a fa-re il sci-mu-ni-to me-stie-re di ma-

*Appoggiatura recommended

62

son, guar - da - te co - sa son, guar - da - te, guar - da - te co - sa

son! Que - ste chia - ma - te de - e, da - gli in - gan - na - ti

sen - si, a cui tri - bu - ta in - cen - si la

de - bo - le ra - gion, la de - bo - le ra - gion, la

de - bo - le ra - gion. Son stre - ghe che in -

can - ta-no per far - ci pe - nar, si - re - ne che

can - ta-no per far - ci af - fo - gar, ci - vet - te che al -

let - ta-no per trar - ci le piu - me, co - me - te che

bril - la - no per to - glier - ci il lu - me; son ro - se spi -

no - se, son vol - pi vez - zo - se, son or - se be -

ni - gne, co - lom - be ma - li - gne, ma - e - stre d'in - gan - ni, a - mi - che d'af -

fan - ni, che fin - go - no, men - to - no. A - mo - re non sen - ton, non sen - ton pie -

son,   co - sa son,   co - sa son! Son stre - ghe che in-can - ta-no, il re - sto nol

di - co, si - re - ne che can - ta-no, il re - sto nol di - co, ci - vet - te che al -

let - ta-no, il re - sto nol di - co, co - me - te che bril - la-no, il re - sto nol

di - co, son ro - se spi - no - se, son vol - pi vez -

68

re - sto, il re - sto nol di - co, già o - gnu - no, già o-gnu-no lo sa.___ Il

re - sto, il re - sto nol di - co, già o - gnu - no, già o-gnu-no lo sa,

già o-gnu - no lo sa, già o-gnu - no lo sa, già o -

gnu - no lo sa.

Madamina! Il catalogo è questo

from
DON GIOVANNI

Wolfgang Amadeus Mozart

me, os - ser - va - te, leg - ge - te con me!

In I - ta - lia sei cen - to e qua - ran - ta,

in Al - ma - gna due cen - to e trent' u - na,

cen - to in Fran - cia, in Tur - chia no - vant' u - na; ma, in I-

spa-gna, ma,in I - spa-gna son già mil-le_e tre, mil-le_e tre,

mil - le_e tre! V'han fra que-ste con-ta - di - ne,

ca - me-rie - re, cit- ta - di - ne, v'han con-tes-se, ba - ro - nes-se,

mar-che-sa - ne, prin-ci - pes - se, e v'han don-ne d'o-gni gra-do,d'o-gni for - ma,d'ogni e-

tà, d'o - gni_ for-ma, d'o - gni e - tà.   In I - ta - lia

sei cen - to e qua-ran - ta,   in Al - ma - gna

due cen - to e trent' u - na,   cen - to in Fran - cia, in Tur-

chia no - vant' u-na; ma, ma,___ ma, in I - spa - gna, ma, in I -

spa-gna son già mil-le e tre, mil-le e tre, mil-le e

tre! V'han fra ques-te con-ta - di - ne, ca-me-rie-re, cit -ta - di - ne, v'han con-tes-se, ba-ro -

nes - se, mar-che-sa - ne, prin - ci - pes-se, e v'han don-ne d'o-gni gra-do, d'o-gni for-ma, d'o-gni e-

tà, d'o - gni for - ma, d'o - gni e -

tà, d'o - gni for - ma, d'o - gni e - tà!

Andante con moto

Nel - la___ bion-da e - gli ha l'u-san - za di lo - dar-la

la gen - ti - lez - za, nel - la bru - na la co-

stan - za, nel - la___ bian - ca la___ dol - cez - za.

ci - na,   la   pic - ci - na, la pic - ci - na, la pic - ci - na, la pic -

ci - na, la pic - ci - na, la pic -ci - na, la pic - ci - na   è o-gnor vez - zo - sa, è o-gnor vez -

zo - sa, è o-gnor vez - zo - sa;   del - le vec -chie fa   con - qui - sta,

pel pia - cer   di por - le in li - sta.   Sua pas-sion pre-do-mi-

78

quel che fa, pur - ché por - ti la gon - nel - la, voi sa -

pe - te quel che fa, voi sa - pe - te, voi sa - pe - te quel che

fa,_____ quel che fa, _____ quel che fa, _____

_ voi sa - pe - te quel che fa.

*The performance tradition is a hum at this spot.

O Isis und Osiris

from
DIE ZAUBERFLÖTE

Wolfgang Amadeus Mozart

In diesen heil'gen Hallen

from
DIE ZAUBERFLÖTE

Wolfgang Amadeus Mozart

1. In die - sen heil' - gen Hal - len kennt
2. In die - sen heil' - gen Mau - ern, wo

man die Ra - che nicht, und ist ein Mensch ge - fal - len, führt
Mensch den Men - schen liebt, kann kein Ver - rä - ter lau - ern, weil

Lie - be ihn zur Pflicht.
man dem Feind ver - gibt.
Dann wan-delt er an Freun - des
Wen sol-che Leh - ren nicht er-

La calunnia

from
IL BARBIERE DI SIVIGLIA

Gioachino Rossini

The aria's original key is D, but transposition down a whole step is so standard that the presentation in C is justified and practical.

che in - sen - si - bi - le e sot - ti - le, leg - ger - men - te, dol - ce -

men - te in - co - min - cia, in - co - min - cia a sus - sur -

rar. Pia - no pia - no,

ter - ra ter - ra, sot - to -

vo - ce si - bi - lan - do

va scor-ren - do, va scor - ren - do, va ron - zan - do, va ron-

zan - do; nell' o - rec - chie del - la gen - te s'in - tro-

du - ce, s'in - tro - du - ce de-stra - men - te, e le te-ste ed i cer - vel - li, e le te-ste ed i cer-

lo - co; sem-bra il tuo-no, la tem - pe - sta che nel sen del - la fo - re - sta va fi - schian-do, bron-to -

lan - do, e ti fa d'or-ror ge - lar. Al - la fin tra-boc - ca e scop - pia, si pro-pa - ga, si rad-

dop - pia e pro-du - ce un'e - splo - sio - ne   co-me un col-po di can -

no - ne, co-me un col-po di can - no - ne, un tre-muo-to, un tem-po-

ra - le, un tre-muo-to, un tem-po - ra - le, un tu-mul-to ge-ne-ra - le che fa l'a-ria rim-bom-

bar, un tre-muo-to, un tem-po - ra - le, un tre-muo-to, un tem-po - ra-le, un tu-mul-to ge-ne-

ra - le che fa l'a-ria rim-bom - bar.

pp

E il me-schi - no ca-lun - nia-to, av-vi-

E il me - schi - no ca - lun - nia - to, av - vi - li - to, cal - pe -

sta - to, sot-to il pub - bli - co fla - gel - lo__ per__ gran__ sor - te__ va a cre -

a piacere *a tempo*

col canto *p a tempo*

par. E il me - schi - no ca - lun - nia - to, av - vi - li - to, cal - pe -

ff

pp

sta - to, sot - to il pub - bli - co fla - gel - lo__ per__ gran__ sor - te__ va a cre -

par, sot - to il pub-bli - co fla - gel -lo per gran sor-te va_a cre - par, sot-to il pub-bli - co fla -

gel - lo per gran sor-te va_a cre - par, sì, va_a cre - par, sì, va_a cre -

par, sì, va_a cre - par.

Miei rampolli femminini

from
LA CENERENTOLA

Gioachino Rossini

Allegro

DON MAGNIFICO:

Miei ram-

pol - li, miei ram-pol - li fem - mi - ni - ni,

vi ri - pu-dio, vi ri-pu-dio; mi ver - go-gno! Un ma-gni - fi - co mio

so-gno mi ve-ni - ste a___ scon - cer - tar,

mi ve-ni - ste a___ scon - cer - tar.___ Vi ri-

pu - dio; mi ver-go-gno! Co-me son mor-ti-fi - ca -

te! De-gne fi-glie d'un ba - ro - ne!

Via: si - len - zio ed at - ten - zio-ne. Sta-te il

so - gno, sta-te il so-gno a me-di - tar.

Mi so-gnai fra il fo-sco e il chia-ro,

mi so-gnai fra il fo-sco e il chia-ro un bel-lis-si-mo so - ma-ro; un so-ma-ro, ma so-

len-ne. Quan-do a un trat-to, oh che por - ten-to! sul-le spal-le a cen-to a

cen - to, sul - le spal-le a cen-to a cen - to gli spun-ta-va-no le pen-ne, gli spun-ta-va-no le

pen - ne, ed in aria, *sciù*, vo - lò! Ed in ci - ma, ed in ci - ma a un cam-pa-

ni - le co-me in tro - no si fer - mò, ed in ci-ma a un cam-pa-ni - le co-me in tro - no si fer-

ec-co il sim-bo-lo spie - ga-to,   ma d'un so-gno s'in-tral - cia-to

ec-co il sim-bo-lo spie - ga-to.   La cam-pa-na suo-na a

p

fe-sta? Al -le-grez-za in ca-sa ques-ta.   Quel-le pen - ne?   Sie -te vo- i.   Quel gran

vo -lo?   Ple-be ad -di-o.   Re-sta l'a - si-no di po-i.   Ma quell' a - si-no son

f   *p*

i - o,   chi vi guar - da   ve - de chia - ro   che il so - ma - ro   è il ge - ni -

tor,   il so-ma-ro è il ge-ni - tor,   il so-ma-ro è il ge-ni - tor.

Fer - ti - lis - si - ma re - gi - na   l'u - na e l'al - tra di - ver -

rà;   ed il non-no u - na doz-zi - na di ram-pol-li ab-brac-cie - rà.   Un re pic - co-lo di

qua... ser - vo, ser - vo, ser - vo, ser - vo; un re bam - bo-lo__ di là... ser - vo, ser - vo, ser - vo,

ser - vo; e la glo - ria mi-a sa - rà, sì, sì, la glo - ria mia sa - rà.

Fer - ti - lis - si - ma re - gi - na l'u - na e l'al - tra di - ver-

rà; ed__ il non-no u-na__doz - zi - na di__ram-pol - li ab-brac-cie - rà. Un re pic - co-lo__ di

qua... ser - vo, ser - vo, ser - vo, ser - vo; un re bam-bo-lo di là... ser - vo, ser - vo, ser - vo,

ser - vo; e la glo-ria mi-a sa - rà, sì, sì, la glo - ria mia sa - rà, un re pic-co-lo qua, un re bam-bo-lo

là, un re pic-co-lo qua, un re bam-bo-lo là, e la glo-ria, e la glo-ria, e la glo-ria mi-a sa-

rà, un re pic-co-lo qua, un re bam-bo-lo là, un re pic-co-lo qua, un re bam-bo-lo là, e la glo-ria, e la

glo - ria, e— la glo-ria mi-a sa-rà, fer - ti-lis-si-ma re-gi - na l'u-na e l'al-tra di-ver-

rà; ed— il non-no u-na-doz-zi-na di— ni-po-ti ab-brac-cie-rà, e la glo-ria mia sa-

rà, e la glo-ria mia sa - rà, mia sa-rà, mia sa - rà, mia sa-rà, mia sa-

rà.

Schweig'! schweig'! damit dich niemand warnt

from
DER FREISCHÜTZ

Carl Maria von Weber

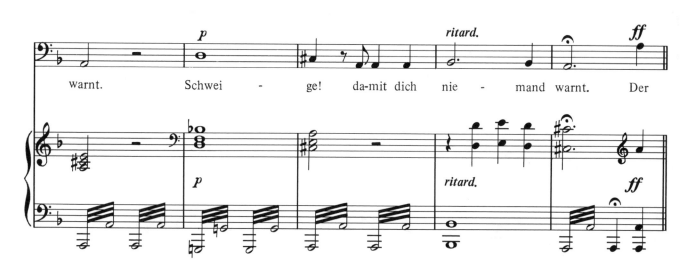

Fall, nichts, nichts vom tie-
fen Fall! Um-gebt ihn, ihr
Gei - ster mit Dun - kel be-schwingt; schon trägt er
knir - schend eu - re Ket - ten! Um-gebt ihn, ihr

Gei - ster mit Dun - kel be - schwingt; schon trägt er

knir - schend eu - re Ket - ten! Tri - umph!

Tri - umph! Tri - umph! Die Ra - che ge -

lingt! Tri - umph! Die Ra - che ge - lingt, die Ra - che, die Ra - che ge -

108

Ra - che ge - lingt! Tri - umph! Tri - umph! _____ Die

Ra - che _____ ge - lingt! Tri - umph! Die Ra - che ge - lingt! Tri -

umph! Die Ra - che ge - lingt!

Vi ravviso

from
LA SONNAMBULA

Vincenzo Bellini

re - ni sì tran-quil - lo i dì pas - sa - i del-la

pri - ma, del - la pri - ma gio - ven - tù! Ca - ri luo - ghi, io vi tro -

vai, ca - ri luo-ghi, io vi tro - va - i, ma quei dì non tro - vo più! Vi rav-

vi - so, o luo-ghi a - me - ni, in cui lie - ti i dì pas-

Ch'io ti mi - ri!   Oh! il va - go vol - to!

col canto

Allegro moderato

p

stent.

Tu non sa - i con quei be - gli oc - chi co - me

dol - ce il cor mi toc - chi, qual ri - chia - mi ai pen - sier

mie - i a - do - ra - bi - le, a - do - ra - bi - le bel - tà. E - ra

des - sa, ah qual tu se - i, sul mat - ti - no, sul mat - ti - no dell' e -

tà, e - ra des - sa, qual tu se - i, sul mat - ti - no dell' e - tà, e - ra des - sa, qual tu

incalz. e rinf. **Più mosso**

se - i, sul mat - ti - no dell' e - tà,_____ dell' e - tà.

incalz. e rinf. **ff** **ff**

Dalle stanza ove Lucia

from
LUCIA DI LAMMERMOOR

Gaetano Donizetti

sor - te, un la - men - to... un gri-do u-sci - a, co - me

d'uom vi - ci - no a mor - te! Cor - si rat - to in quel - le

mu - ra... ahi! ter - ri - bi - le scia - gu - ra! Ste-so Ar-

tu - ro al suol gia - ce - va mu - to, fred - do, in-san-gui-

120

men-te la__vir-tu-de_a lei_man-cò,   a le - - i,   a lei,   in-fe-

li - ce,in-fe-li-ce! del-la men-te la vir-tu-de_a lei man-cò!   ah!

Maestoso

Ah! quel - la de - stra di san - gue im-

pu - ra l'i - ra non chia - mi su noi del ciel.

Ah! quel - la de - stra di san - gue im - pu - ra

l'i - ra non chia - mi su noi del ciel. El - la in

me le lu - ci_af - fis - se, e l'ac - ciar, l'ac-ciar strin-

ge - va!

Ah! Ah! quel - la de - stra

di_san-gue_im-pu - ra l'i - ra non chia - mi su noi del

Pour les couvents c'est fini

(Piff, paff)

from

LES HUGUENOTS

Giacomo Meyerbeer

Vo-lon-tiers, un vieil air hu-gue-not con-tre les gens du pape et le sex-e dam-na - ble; vous le con-nais-sez bien— c'est notre air des com-

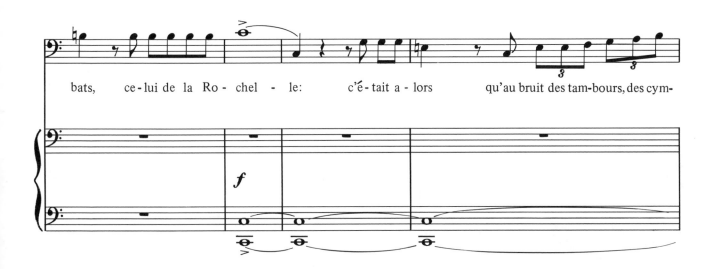

bats, ce-lui de la Ro-chel - le: c'é-tait a-lors qu'au bruit des tam-bours, des cym-

ba - les, ac - com - pa - gné du piff, paff, pouff des bal - les je chan - tais, je chan -

Allegretto

tais: piff, paff, piff, paff.

Pour les cou - vents c'est fi - ni, les

moi - nes à ter - re; guerre à tout ca - got bé - ni, pa - pis - tes la

guer - re. Li - vrons____ à la _ flamme aux fers leurs tem _ ples d'en -

fer, li - vrons_____ leurs_ tem - ples d'en - fer,_____

cresc.

p

li - vrons leurs tem - ples, tem - ples d'en - fer;_____ ter -

p

ras - sons_les, cer - nons_les, frap-pons_les, per - çons_les, ter -

f

ras - sons—les, cer-nons—les, frap-pons—les, per-çons—les,

piff, paff, pouff, cer - nons—les, piff, paff, pouff, frap-pons — les,

piff, paff, pouff, piff, paff, piff, paff, pouff, piff. Qu'ils

pleu - rent, qu'ils meu - rent, mais grâ - ce ja - mais, qu'ils

131

Ah! un foco insolito

from
DON PASQUALE

Gaetano Donizetti

DON PASQUALE:

Ah! _____ un fo-co in-so-li-to mi sen-to ad-dos-so, o-mai re-

si-ste-re io più non pos-so. Dell' e-tà vec-chia scor-do i ma-lan-ni,

mi sen-to gio-vi-ne co-me a vent' an-ni. Deh! ca-ra, af-fret-ta-ti! Vie-ni, spo-

dos - so, o ca - sco mor - to qua.

Ah! _____ un fo - co in - so - li - to

mi sen - to ad - dos - so, o - mai re - si - ste - re io più non pos - so. Dell' e - tà

vec - chia scor - do i ma - lan - ni, mi sen - to gio - vi - ne co - me a vent'

138

Infelice! e tuo credevi

from
ERNANI

Giuseppe Verdi

no - re, dell' on - ta che si re - ca al suo si - gno - re.

Andante

In - fe - li - ce! e tuo cre - de - vi sì bel gi - glio im - ma - co -

la - to! Del tuo cri - ne fra le ne - vi piom - ba in - ve - ce, piom - ba in - ve - ce il di - so -

nor. Ah, per - ché, per - ché _ l'e - ta - de in se - no gio - vin co - re _____ m'ha_ ser-

ba - to! Mi do - ve - van gli an - ni al - me - no far di ge - lo, far di ge - lo an - co - ra il

cor, far di_ ge - lo an - co - ra il cor, far____ di_ ge - lo____ an - co - ra il

cor, mi do - ve - van gli an - ni al - me - no far__ di ge - lo, far di ge - lo an - co - ra il

cor, an - co - ra il cor, an - co - ra, an - co - ra il cor.

Come dal ciel precipita

from
MACBETH

Giuseppe Verdi

Adagio ($\bullet$ = 56)

Co - me dal ciel pre - ci - pi - ta l'om - bra più sem - pre_o-

scu - ra! In not - te_u - gual tra - fis - se - ro Dun - ca - no, il mio si-

gnor. Mil - le_af - fan - no - se_im-

ma - gi - ni m'an - nun - cia - no sven - tu - ra,

146

Als Büblein klein

from
DIE LUSTIGEN WEIBER VON WINDSOR

Otto Nicolai

mir die Kan - ne her, füll' mir den Schlauch!

Lösch' mir der Keh - le __ Brand, Trin - ken ist kei - ne __ Schand';

Ba - chus trank auch, ja! Ba - chus trank __ auch! *Nun in Positur!*

Hal-tet Euch be-reit! Macht die Keh-len weit!

rall.　　　　　　　　　　　　Adagio

führt　es　nach　Haus,　ja!　　führt　es　nach＿ Haus.　*Nun in Positur!*

p rall.　　　　　　　　　　pp

Allegro con fuoco

f

Hal-tet　Euch　be-reit!　　　　　Macht die Keh-len weit!

f　sf　　　　　　　f　sf

Presto

Eins,　zwei und　drei!

ff

sf　sf　sf　sf　sf　sf

O tu, Palermo

from
I VESPRI SICILIANI

Giuseppe Verdi

O pa - tria, o ca-ra pa-tria, al-fin, al-fin ti veg-go! L'e - su-le ti sa-

lu - ta do-po sì lun - ga as-sen - za.   Il fio-

ren - te tuo suo-lo ri - pien d'a-mo-re io ba-cio,   recco il mio vo-to a

te, re-co il mi-o vo-to a te col brac-cio e il co — re!

Largo (♩ = 40)

p dolcissimo

p cantabile

O tu, Pa-

stent.
morendo

pp

ler — mo, ter-ra a-do-ra-ta, a — me sì ca-ro — ri-so d'a-

allarg.   *dim.*

mor, ah! al-za la fron — te tan-to ol-trag-gia-ta, il tuo ri-

col canto

pi - glia pri - mier splen - dor,＿ il＿tu-o ri - pi - glia pri-mier,＿pri-mier＿splen-

dor! Chie-si a i - ta a stra-nie - re na-

zio - ni, ra-min-gai per ca-stel - la e cit-

tà; ma in - sen - si - bil al fer - vi - do

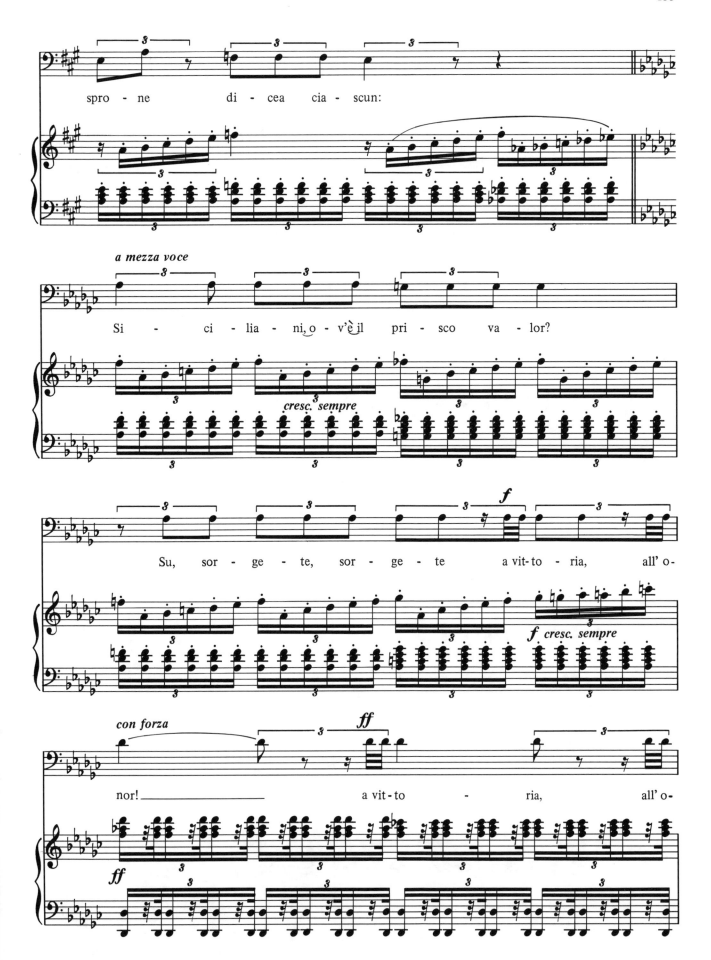

nor! _____ a vit - to - ria, all'o - nor! O tu, Pa-

ler - mo, ter - ra a - do - ra - ta, a ____ me sì

ca - ro _____ ri - so d'a - mor, ah! _____ al - za la

fron - te tan - to ol - trag - gia - ta, il ____ tu - o ri-

Il lacerato spirito

from
SIMON BOCCANEGRA

Giuseppe Verdi

Il la - ce - ra - to spi - ri - to del me - sto ge - ni - to - re

e - ra ser - ba-to a stra - zio d'in - fa-mia e di do - lo - re.

II

ser - to a lei de' mar - ti - ri pie - to - so il cie - lo diè.

Le veau d'or

from
FAUST

Charles Gounod

MÉPHISTOPHÉLÈS:

1. Le veau d'or _____ est tou-jours de - bout! On en-
2. Le veau d'or _____ est vain-queur des dieux! Dans sa

cen - se sa puis - san - - - ce, on en -
gloi - re dé - ri - soi - - - re, dans sa

cen - se sa puis - san - - - ce d'un bout du
gloi - re dé - ri - soi - - - re le mon-stre ab-

monde à l'au - tre bout! Pour fê - ter l'in-fâme i -
ject in-sulte aux cieux! Il con - temple, ô rage é -

pp

do - le, rois et peu - ples con - fon - dus, au bruit
tran - ge! à ses pieds le genre hu - main, se ru -

som - bre des é - cus, dan - sent u - ne ron - de
ant, le fer en main, dans le sang et dans la

Vous qui faites l'endormie

from
FAUST

Charles Gounod

MÉPHISTOPHÉLÈS:

Vous qui fai - tes l'en - dor - mi - e, n'en - ten - dez - vous pas, _____

n'en - ten - dez - vous pas, ô Ca - the - ri - ne, ma mi - e, n'en - ten - dez - vous

pas   ma voix et mes pas?_____   Ain - si ton ga - lant t'ap -

pel - le,_____   ain - si ton ga - lant t'ap - pel - le,_____

et ton cœur   l'en   croit.   Ah! ah! ah!   ah! ah! ah! ah! ah! ah!

ah!   N'ou-vre ta por - te, ma bel - le,   que la bague au_____

doigt, n'ou - vre ta por - te, ma bel - le, que la bague au

doigt, que la bague au doigt!

poco meno mosso

Ca - the - ri - ne que j'a -

do - re, pour-quoi re - fu - ser, _____ pour - quoi re - fu - ser

à l'a - mant qui vous im - plo - re, pour-quoi re - fu - ser un si doux bai -

ser?_____ Ain - si ton ga - lant sup - pli - e,_____

ain - si ton ga - lant sup - pli - e,_____ et ton cœur l'en

croit. Ah! ah! ah! ah! ah! ah! ah! ah! ah! ah!

Quand la flamme de l'amour

from
LA JOLIE FILLE DE PERTH

Georges Bizet

Più andante ($\downarrow$. = 40)

Quand la flam-me de l'a-mour brû - le l'â - me nuit et jour, pour l'é - tein-dre quel-que-fois,

sans me plain-dre, moi je bois! Je ris! Je chan - te! Je ris,— je chan-te et — je

bois! Tra la la la la la la la la la la— Tra la la la la!

Ah! tra la la_____ tra la la_____ tra la la_____ la la!_____

S'il est u-ne tris-te fo-li - e, c'est cel - le d'un pauvre a-mou-

reux___ qu'un re-gard de femme hu-mi - li - e, qu'un mot peut ren-dre mal - heu-

reux,_ qu'un re - gard de femme hu - mi - li - e, qu'un mot peut ren-dre mal - heu-

reux,_ hé - las!_____ Quand on ai - me sans es - poir,_

Gremin's Aria

from
EUGENE ONEGIN

Pyotr Il'yich Tchaikovsky

Più mosso, quasi allegro (♩ = 108)

Lyrics (vocal line):

СОЛНЦА ЛУЧ СРЕ-ДИ НЕ - НА-СТЬЯ, МНЕ ЖИЗНЬ И МО - ЛО-ДОСТЬ, ДА,

МО - ЛО-ДОСТЬ И СЧАС — — ТЬЕ! СРЕ - ДИ ЛУ -

КА - ВЫХ, МА - ЛО-ДУШ - НЫХ, МАЛЬ - НЫХ, БА -

ЛО - ВАН-НЫХ ДЕ - ТЕЙ, ЗЛО - ДЕ-ЕВ И СМЕШ - НЫХ, И

СКУЧ - НЫХ, ТУ - ПЫХ, ПРИ - ВЯЗ - ЧИ-ВЫХ СУ - ДЕЙ; СРЕ-ДИ КО -

КЕ - ТОК БО - ГО - МОЛЬНЫХ, СРЕ - ДИ ХО - ЛОП - ЕВ ДО - БРО -

ВОЛЬ - НЫХ, СРЕ - ДИ ВСЕ - ДНЕВ-НЫХ МОДНЫХ СЦЕН, УЧ - ТИ - ВЫХ,

Meno mosso (♩ = 88)

ЛАС - КОВЫХ ИЗ - МЕН; СРЕ - ДИ ХО - ЛОД-НЫХ ПРИ-ГО -

В СИ-ЯНЬ-И АН - ГЕ-ЛА, В СИ-ЯНЬ-И АН - ГЕ-ЛА ЛУ - ЧИС-ТОМ!

Tempo I (♩ = 66)

ЛЮБ - ВИ ВСЕ ВОЗ-РАС-ТЫ ПО - КОР-НЫ,

Е - ё ПО - РЫ-ВЫ БЛА-ГО - ТВОР-НЫ И

Ю - НО-ШЕ В РАС-ЦВЕ - ТЕ ЛЕТ ЕД-ВА У - ВИ-ДЕВ-ШЕ-МУ СВЕТ,

И ЗА-КА-ЛЁН-НО-МУ СУДЬ-БОЙ БОЙ-ЦУ С СЕ-ДО-Ю ГО-ЛО-

ВОЙ. О-НЕ-ГИН, Я СКРЫ-ВАТЬ НЕ

СТА-НУ, БЕЗ-УМ-НО Я ЛЮ-БЛЮ ТАТЬ-Я-НУ!

a piena voce

ТОС-КЛИ-ВО ЖИЗНЬ МО-Я ТЕК-ЛА, О-НА Я-ВИ-ЛАСЬ И ДА-

Épouse quelque brave fille

from
MANON

Jules Massenet

Les grands mots que voi - là! Quel - le route as - tu donc sui -

vi - e, et que sais-tu de cet-te vi - e pour pen - ser qu'el-le fi-nit là?

É - pou - se quel-que bra - ve fil - le

di - gne de nous, di - gne de toi;_____ de - viens un pè - re de fa -

mil - le ni pi - re, ni meil - leur que moi: le ciel n'en veut pas da - van -

ta - ge. C'est là le de - voir, en - tends - tu? C'est là le de -

voir!_____ La ver - tu qui fait du ta - pa - ge n'est dé - jà plus de la ver -

Vecchia zimarra, senti

from
LA BOHÈME

Giacomo Puccini

COLLINE:

Vec - chia zi - mar - ra, sen - ti, io re-sto al pian, tu a -

scen - de-re il sa-cro mon-te or de - vi. Le mie gra - zie ri - ce - vi.

Mai non cur - va - sti il lo - go-ro dor-so ai ric-chi ed ai po-ten - ti.

Pas - sar nel-le tue ta - sche co - me_in an - tri tran-

quil - li fi-lo-so-fi_e po - e - ti. O - ra che_i gior-ni lie - ti fug-gir, ti_

di - co ad-di - o, fe-de-le_a-mi-co mi - o,_____ ad - dio,___ ad-

dio.

Let things be like they always was

from
STREET SCENE

Kurt Weill

What what is it

from
THE MOTHER OF US ALL

Virgil Thomson